CHRISTIANITY UNPLUGGED

"Following Jesus Beyond the Construct of Religion"

Written By

ERIC D. CANADAY

Christianity Unplugged
Following Jesus beyond the construct of religion

www.ChristianityUnplugged.com

Copyright © 2009 by Eric D.Canaday
All rights reserved

Except for brief excerpts for review purposes, no part of this book may be reproduced in any form, stored in a retrieval system, or transmitted in any form by any means — electronic, mechanical, photocopy, recording, or otherwise — without prior written permission of the publisher, except as provided by United States of America copyright law.

Published by Inner Witness Media, Inc.
Aurora, Colorado

Except where otherwise indicated, all Scripture quotations are from the Holy Bible, New International Version. Copyright © 1973, 1978, 1984 by the International Bible Society. Used by permission of Zondervan Bible Publishers.

Printed in the United States of America
Second Edition

Connect with Eric Canaday at:
www.ChristianityUnplugged.net
www.twitter.com/ericcanaday
www.facebook.com/ericcanaday

ISBN: 978-0-6153070-3-9

Dedication

To those outside of the
camp who love God and
know that they have been called
according to His purpose.

Hebrews 13:12-14

Table of Contents

Preface – Christianity?..7

Chapter 1 - Unplugged..13

Chapter 2 - Understanding The Gospel...............23

Chapter 3 - Called to the ministry........................ 35

Chapter 4 - A revolution in worship....................53

Chapter 5 – The Truth About Tithing...................65

Chapter 6 - Getting out of the boat.......................73

Chapter 7 – Life after Religion..............................83

Epilogue - You don't have to be perfect.............107

CHRISTIANITY UNPLUGGED

– Preface –

CHRISTIANITY?

No servant can serve two masters. Either he will hate the one and love the other, or he will be devoted to the one and despise the other.
You cannot serve both God and money.

-Luke 16:13

Eric D. Canaday

Christianity Unplugged

This book captures my criticisms of Christianity and I respect that some who hold this religion in high regard may not embrace my point of view. I am sharing this information to empower believers who are interested in pursuing a vibrant relationship with God without relying on clerical dogma or temple-based worship. I want them to know that they do not have to perform for *people* to receive *God's* love and acceptance. If that sounds like the most heretical thing you have ever heard, this book may not be for you.

Still, I invite you to hear me out, from beginning to end, and I ask that you measure my words in light of the truth revealed in the scriptures. I thank you in advance for your empathy.

To begin, Christianity is a political system that generates revenue by charging its members for access to God through a temple that is frequently referred to as the "local church." Like many religions, adherents must contribute their offerings of time, talent, and money to an ordained minister in exchange for God's blessings. Larger Christian denominations have streamlined this model through franchising and they have training centers called seminaries where franchisees (ordained ministers) can learn how to maintain a steady flow of income.

The greatest benefit of these franchises is that they are excellent gathering places that satisfy our need for inspiration and community. Many of them are charitable, and congregants are usually able to see the benefits of pooling their resources to help those in need.

However, the underlying notion of this social construct is that money controlled in the name of

Jesus is the solution to the world's woes. The fatal flaw in this thinking is that it assumes Jesus established the Church to consolidate wealth into the hands of clerical rulers who have the divine right to govern the world on his behalf. This notion is absolutely false.

Establishing the kingdom of God on earth has nothing to do with constructing houses of worship or collecting money. God created the universe, so he does not need for us to acquire property or land on his behalf. The only territory where God does not exercise sovereign authority is in the domain of the human heart. He sent his son Jesus Christ to establish his kingdom within this domain and that kingdom is advancing through the *power of love.* Christianity is unplugged, because it seeks to establish God's kingdom on earth through the *economic power* that it derives from the combined wealth of its adherents.

Within Christianity I was let to believe that God loved me only as long as I was willing to fuel the system of religious control with my personal resources. I have since learned that my value to God is far greater than being a battery or a cog within a religious machine. That said the goal of this book is not to reform or dismantle Christianity. I believe that it will exist until Jesus returns for *The* Church. My goal is to let people know that they do not have to live within its confines.

- 1 -

Unplugged

They have lost connection with the head, from whom the whole body, supported and held together by its ligaments and sinews, grows as God causes it to grow.

- Colossians 2:19, TNIV

Eric D. Canaday

Christianity Unplugged

The word "Christianity" does not appear in the bible. However, it has become a religious system of social order that provides regulations for moral conduct and rituals for worship. It is generally accepted that in order to be a good "Christian" a person must:

- Accept Jesus Christ as their savior
- Become a member of the local church
- Participate in weekly worship services
- Give tithes and offerings
- Volunteer
- Pray, read the Bible, live a moral life
- And invite people to church

This is not an all-inclusive list, but these are a few acceptable attributes of a person who has converted to the "Christian religion."

Since the Edict of Milan, our institutions have spent billions of dollars constructing edifices for worship. We have sent missionaries into the world to ask the "lost" to become members of our organizations; making it clear that their decision will save them from God's judgment and impending wrath. To date, we have also established more than 38,000 denominational Christian sects in order to meet the diverse cultural needs of our ecclesiastical community. As a result of this effort, Christianity has become the largest religion on the planet, laying claim to over 2.1 billion adherents worldwide.

The challenge in all of this is that Jesus did not come to establish a new religious system. He also never told his followers to build temples so that we could fill them up with people who had converted to the Christian faith.

He told his followers to make disciples and show them how to follow one simple command. In John 13:34-36 Jesus said:

Christianity Unplugged

A new command I give you: love one another. As I have loved you, so you must love one another. By this all men will know that you are my disciples, if you love one another.

One of the core problems with Christianity is that Christians in general are not known for their love. The divisions in the Church based upon race, culture, class, dogma, and clergy power-politics indicates that collectively Christianity has lost its way. This hypocrisy undermines the credibility of Jesus' message and now is the time for change.

For much of my adult life my entire identity was wrapped up in the idea of being a "good church going Christian." Like many believers, I thought it was my duty to conform to this construct. But after studying the bible for myself, I discovered that I had become a Christian who had never truly become a disciple of Jesus Christ. I knew how to follow all of the clerical rules, but I knew very little about following Jesus or walking with him in the way of love.

In my disillusionment with this truth, I started a blog and wrote the following post titled, "Tired of Church." It reads:

What comes to mind when someone mentions the word church? For most of us a church is a building where you go to worship or serve God. Most people go to church to get the answers that they need to deal with their personal problems.

Participating in church related activities has always given me a sense of closeness to other believers and refreshing in the Lord. I am the first to admit that a good sermon can provide the perspective needed to overcome the adversity we face in life. I have lead praise and worship, served as a deacon, taught Sunday school, and performed in several church plays. However, I have a confession to make... I am tired of what we call church.

Before I get too far along in this article I need to make it clear that I am not recommending a mass exodus from traditional "churches." God has called us to unity and the last thing that I want to do is add to the damage that has already been done. However, Church is not a building, a Christian social club, or a registered non-profit corporation. It is a worldwide community of people who have committed their lives to sharing the love of Jesus Christ everyday!

I have spent the last 25 years "going" to church and I am tired of the routine. I long for something so much more. I want every member the body of Christ to know that they have the power to make a difference. I want them to find the courage to take action.

I want us to be the Church..."

Shortly after posting the article I made a decision to unplug my life, my money, and my voluntary service from the system of religion known as Christianity. When I walked away, I felt like a weight had been lifted. That is, until a friend of mine confronted me about my article. He said:

Now that you have created this article; what will the solution be? Because you will be asked; also, how do we break the tradition of church? You and I know that Church is really about community, but so often churches grow larger than their communities. We have been taught to have faith rather than a realistic effort. What do we do to change that? You know some people believe more in tithing/giving 10% rather than living right. We need a solution Eric.

My initial feeling was that we needed to go to the preachers and tell them to stop utilizing ordination and temple-based worship to mediate the relationship between God and his people. But that would be a ridiculous request because ordained clerics generate revenue for their organizations by teaching these principles. Asking them to do something this drastic would be like asking America to relinquish its dependence on foreign oil. Its not going to happen any time soon.

Christianity Unplugged

After giving it some additional thought I came to the conclusion that Christianity cannot be fixed; but it can be transcended. Jesus Christ is not the founder of Christianity anyway. It is a political system of worship that proliferates only because 2.1 billion people agree to behave as if it exists (for details about the origins of Christianity I highly encourage you to read Pagan Christianity by Frank Viola and George Barna).

The solution lies in embracing the fact that we have God's permission to let go of a religion in order to follow his Son in the way of love.

Eric D. Canaday

Understanding the Gospel

*But now a righteousness from God, apart from law,
has been made known,
to which the Law and the Prophets testify.*

- Romans 3:21

Eric D. Canaday

CHRISTIANITY UNPLUGGED

I began attending worship services consistently around the age of 8 after one of the neighbors asked my mother if she could take me and my sister to Sunday school. I enjoyed going because it was a time where I could hang out with my neighborhood friends (and as I grew older, I found that it was a good place to meet girls).

Normally class would meet for about 30 minutes and we would read bible stories and answer questions from the teachers guide book. Afterward, the teachers would gather the 4th through 6th grade classes for a final review of the day's lesson. It was during this time that they would share the "gospel" with us.

Here is how I comprehended the message:

> *We are all sinners who were born in sin. If we die in our sins we will go to hell to be tortured by the devil forever. God does not want anyone to die and burn in hell, so he sent his son Jesus to die on the cross for our sins. John 3:16 (KJV) says "For God so loved the world, that he gave his only begotten Son, that whosoever believeth in him should not perish, but have everlasting life"*
>
> *God raised Jesus from the dead and he is now in heaven waiting for us. If you accept Jesus today, when you die, you are guaranteed a place with Jesus in the paradise of heaven…forever!*

After they shared the "good news" they would give us an opportunity to join the church by walking up to the front of the class to accept Jesus as our lord and savior.

That message instilled the fear of God in me! I think I wanted to accept Jesus the first time I heard it, but I was more afraid of looking like a nerd in front of the classroom than I was of hell. I finally made my decision at the age of 11 after my friend Phil agreed to go up and "Get Saved" with me. I was overjoyed when I finally got baptized. When I came up out of the water I felt like something had changed for the better. The sad part of this story is that I did not become a Christian because of my love for God. I also had no concept of his genuine love for me. I became a Christian because I was afraid of hell.

A year later, when I was about 12 years old, my parents were going through a divorce. Even before my father left he was rarely home and I always missed him. One day I came home from school, walked into the bathroom, and noticed that all of my father's toiletries were missing from the counter of the sink. Intuition told me that something was wrong so I rushed downstairs to check his closet. When I opened the door and saw that every stitch of his clothing was gone, I literally wanted to die. I wanted to commit suicide but I was too afraid of hell to take my own life. Never the less, the emotional pain that I felt shook my faith.

That night as I cried in the darkness of my room I asked God, "Why are we born to go through hell, only to die and go to Heaven?" They told me in Sunday school that God sent Jesus so that when I died, I could go to heaven and live peacefully with God. It seemed logical to me that it would be better to skip hell on earth. I was ready for paradise.

No more pain...

    No more rejection...

        No more disappointment.

I figured my current suffering was nothing compared to the hell-fire I was told I would face for all eternity if I committed the sin of self-murder. So every night for almost a year I would just pray, frequently asking God to take me to heaven while I slept. Thankfully, He did not grant my request.

The fact remains that the gospel I heard was not the "good news" preached in the Bible. It was actually a coercive threat structured to purchase my institutional obedience through fear. The problem with the gospel that has been preached is that it misrepresents God's plan for peace.

In the beginning, God gave mankind the power of self-governance or free will. With this freedom we obtained the ability to choose the way of love (which leads to joy, peace, and life) or the way of hate (which leads to fear, violence, and death). Historically mankind has chosen a policy of hate in our dealings with one another. It is this choice that is the source of much of the suffering and injustice that we experience in our world. Our failure to love is what the Bible calls sin.

Governments and religious institutions have tried and faltered in their effort to implement peace for the world's citizens. God sent his son Jesus to show us how to reconcile our differences. His plan was to mediate peace through the power of love. This "Good News" is outlined in 1 John 4:9-17. It says:

"This is how God showed his love among us: He sent his one and only Son into the world that we might live through him. This is love: not that we loved God, but that he loved us and sent his Son as an atoning sacrifice for our sins. Dear friends, since God so loved us, we also ought to love one another. No one has ever seen God; but if we love one another,
God lives in us and
his love is made complete in us.
We know that we live in him and he in us, because he has given us of his Spirit. And we have seen and testify that the Father has sent his Son to be the Savior of the world. If anyone acknowledges that Jesus is the Son of God, God lives in him and he in God.
And so we know and rely on
the love God has for us.
God is love. Whoever lives in love lives in God, and God in him. In this way, love is made

complete among us so that we will have confidence on the Day of Judgment, because in this world we are like him."

This version of the gospel may be hard to swallow for some people because religion has conditioned us to believe that we had to follow a bunch of religious laws to be righteous in God's eyes. It also lacks the dogmatic fear tactic of making people think that believing in Jesus Christ is a matter of choosing between eternal bliss in heaven or eternal torture in hell. This understanding is vitally important because to effectively communicate the "good news" you must be clear on what it is.

The "good news" is -- through God's son Jesus Christ we can receive righteousness, loving acceptance into the family of God, and eternal life without conforming to external religious rules and regulations. God's plan is to free us from the fear of punishment by transforming our hearts from the inside out! God's expectations are not dictated by multilayered legal codes or people pleasing. Jesus gave his life to free us from the power that the law of reciprocity had over our lives. If we believe in him, God forgives us for every unloving or shameful thing that we have done. Romans 3:22-28 sums it up:

This righteousness from God comes through faith in Jesus Christ to all who believe. There is no difference, for all have sinned and fall short of the glory of God, and are justified freely by his grace through the redemption that came by Christ Jesus. God presented him as a sacrifice of atonement, through faith in his blood. He did this to demonstrate his justice, because in his forbearance he had left the sins committed beforehand unpunished – he did it to demonstrate his justice at the present time, so as to be just and the one who justifies those who have faith in Jesus.

Where, then, is boasting? It is excluded. On what principle? On that of observing the law? No, but on that of faith.

Christianity Unplugged

For we maintain that a man is justified by faith apart from observing the law.

Eric D. Canaday

– 3 –

Called to the Ministry

The harvest is plentiful, but the workers are few. Ask the Lord of the harvest, therefore, to send out workers into his harvest field.

- Luke 10:2

Eric D. Canaday

Christianity Unplugged

In 2007, two nationally known evangelists announced that they were divorcing their husbands. What was disheartening is that both of them were married to men who were the pastors of congregations that had several thousand members. The question that immediately came to mind was,

"How in the heck can you be a professional minister who helps people with their life issues, and then fail to hold your marriage together?"

It did not make much sense to me at the time. But now I understand how it could happen.

Ministries are normally started when an individual, or a couple receives what they believe is a vision to accomplish a specific task for God. While the strategies often differ, the common goal is to preach the gospel to sinners so that their souls can be "saved" from the fires of hell. In certain denominations, people who feel called to the "soul saving" ministry are required to go to seminary to obtain the qualifications needed to become a ruler in one of the party's pre-established congregations.

In non-denominational circles, the prospective pastor will usually notify his family and friends of his "call" to the ministry and begin holding Bible studies of some sort. As the group begins to grow the new pastor will begin collecting tithes and offerings to cover his salary, the building fund, and the cost of incorporating the new ministry. In the beginning, there are very few paid employees of the burgeoning non-profit organization. So, the pastor will usually ordain a few ministers and deacons who have proven that they are loyal to him and the vision of the organization. Usually these people are either the family or close friends of the pastor and the title will satisfy them for some time.

CHRISTIANITY UNPLUGGED

As the organization begins to gain momentum, the pastor will frequently communicate sermons that are tied to his vision and direction of the community. The members are encouraged to share the vision with their family, friends, and co-workers so that they too can be a part of all that God is doing in their up and coming organization.

In order to maintain the momentum the pastor will implement a Sunday school program, and if possible, develop a strong choir or praise and worship team. These elements are critical to future growth because most people who attend worship services on a frequent basis will not stay in a congregation that does not have good preaching, a children's ministry and inspirational music. New members are the lifeblood of any new fellowship so it is important that the ministry has programs that will attract and retain them.

If the pastor and his wife are charismatic and they have strong leadership, marketing and administrative abilities, they should find success in building a strong and vibrant Christian fellowship. Hopefully the congregation will be full of loyal members who provide the financial support needed to expand the gospel message all over the world through conferences, radio broadcasts, television, the Internet and other media.

The formula for "church planting" success is:

This scenario creates a win-win situation for both the clergy and the laity because when both classes go to heaven God will give an equal blessing to everyone who participated in the winning of the souls. In a sense the, whole system is like God's very own 401K retirement plan. It may not pay very much during this life but the returns are out of this world!!!

Or so we have been led to believe...

Christianity Unplugged

For most of my adult life, I gladly contributed 10% of my income to these types of retirement plans looking forward to the day when God would say, *"Well done my good and faithful servant."* That is until I realized that Jesus never called anyone to start this kind of soul-saving ministry. Why? Because it's too bureaucratic and almost impossible for the ordinary person to duplicate.

The bureaucracy is great for those in power. But it oppresses the will of the attendees who have been led to believe that inviting people to a worship service and living vicariously through a preacher is the most effective way for them to participate in the ministry.

In contrast, Jesus spent most of his time in ministry with people who were not welcome in the temple. In scripture you never see Jesus or his disciples inviting people to become a member of the local synagogue. Jesus invited people into a restored relationship with God. This work is what the bible calls "the ministry of reconciliation". In 2 Corinthians 5:13-21 Paul the apostle said:

> Christ's love compels us, because we are convinced that one died for all, and therefore all died. And he died for all, that those who live should no longer live for themselves but for him who died for them and was raised again. So from now on we regard no one from a worldly point of view. Though we once regarded Christ in this way, we do so no longer. Therefore, if anyone is in Christ, he is a new creation; the old has gone, the new has come! All this is from God, who reconciled us to himself through Christ and gave us the ministry of reconciliation:
> that God was reconciling the world to himself in Christ, not counting men's sins against them. And he has committed to us the message of reconciliation. We are therefore Christ's ambassadors, as though God were making his appeal through us. We implore you on Christ's behalf: Be reconciled to God. God made him

*who had no sin to be sin for us, so that in him
we might become the righteousness of God.*

This verse begins by saying that Christ's love compels us. It ends by saying he has committed to us the message of reconciliation. Jesus is the Savior of the world, but he did not give us the ministry of "saving souls." He gave each of us the ministry of reconciliation.

The reason why a pastor and his wife can get a divorce while serving as the leaders of a Christian organization is because they have lost sight of the true ministry of Jesus. The ability to build a large congregation is not the sign of God's blessing. Being reconciled and then teaching others to do the same is the ministry that matters. In fairness, reconciliation takes 2 people who are willing to acknowledge that harm has been done in the past, but they are willing to move forward without repeating the same transgressions. This precept is not effectively taught or exemplified within Christianity so we should be prayerful and gracious in our assessments of individuals who falter in this area.

Let me shift gears here and say that I believe that respect is the assumption of equality. The current separation being made in the body of Christ between clergy and laity is the pinnacle of disrespect. This caste system undercuts the right of every believer to participate with Jesus Christ in his ministry without the approval of an ordained cleric.

Jesus governs the Church through the power of the Holy Spirit by one rule…love. Christian institutions on the other hand govern through a multilayered system of by-laws and traditions. There is no scriptural justification for the hierarchal structures of superiority we find in today's denominations. Jesus did not give anyone ruling authority over the flock! Here's is where Jesus made this clear to the first disciples:

Christianity Unplugged

> *You know that the rulers of the Gentiles lord it over them, and their high officials exercise authority over them.* **Not so with you.** *Instead, whoever wants to become great among you must be your servant, and whoever wants to be first must be your slave — just as the Son of Man did not come to be served, but to serve, and to give his life as a ransom for many*
> *- Matthew 20:25-28.*

Kings sit on thrones and judges sit on platforms. Modern day clerics speak down to congregants from elevated pulpits. Many preachers expect the common people to acknowledge them by their titles and they love to be honored during pastor's appreciation events. Jesus made a similar observation about the disrespectful religious leaders of his day in Matthew 23:5-12

> *Everything they do is done for men to see: They make their phylacteries wide and the tassels on their garments long; they love the place of honor at banquets and the most*

important seats in the synagogues; they love to be greeted in the marketplaces and to have men call them 'Rabbi.' But you are not to be called 'Rabbi,' **for you have only one Master and you are all brothers.** *And do not call anyone on earth 'father,' for you have one Father, and he is in heaven. Nor are you to be called 'teacher,' for you have one Teacher, the Christ. The greatest among you will be your servant. For whoever exalts himself will be humbled, and whoever humbles himself will be exalted.*

Jesus compared godly leaders to the people that serve food at your local restaurant. Our leaders are servants, not administrative governors. This may be the reason that Jesus only instructed Peter to feed his sheep (see John 21:17 and Jeremiah 3:15)

Ephesians 4:11 says that Jesus...

> *...gave some to be apostles, some prophets, some evangelists, and some pastors and teachers, for the equipping of the saints for the work of ministry.*

This scripture does not say that our leaders start a ministry and fill it with souls. It says that our leaders are responsible for teaching the saints to participate with Jesus in the ministry of reconciliation.

We have handicapped ourselves by classifying ministry as a soul-saving program, a worship event, or an organization lead by an ordained minister. It only works if people are willing to come to the temple, join the association, and participate in the "ministry" being offered. Jesus established a simpler strategy. He called every single one of his disciples to participate with him in his ministry. If you are a follower of Jesus Christ he is calling you. Here is what he is asking you to do:

> *...go and make disciples of all nations, baptizing them in the name of the Father and of the Son and of the Holy Spirit, and teaching them to obey everything I have commanded you. And surely I am with you always, to the very end of the age.*
>
> *- Matthew 28:19-20*

A disciple is someone that believes the gospel (see chapter 2), gets baptized, and makes being a loving person their highest ambition. They don't give people a sales pitch about heaven or condemn them to hell if they don't convert. They also don't try to convince people that they are right by beating them over the head with the bible. They simply build authentic relationships with the people in their sphere of influence and share God's love through their actions. They communicate the message of reconciliation only after they have earned the right to be heard.

Making disciples happens most effectively within the context of community. If you are not connected in relationship to other believers, making disciples, and helping them to become mature in God's love could be challenging. Still, there are people all around you that are struggling in their lives because of fear, guilt, and shame. A few of them would love to know that God cares. Since there is a strong likely hood that a professional minister is not going to show up and relay this message, Jesus Christ is sending you.

If you think about it, the people who have made the greatest impact in your life were ordinary people. God sent them to you when you needed them and they helped you find your way. Their only agenda was to care for you in a moment, or for a lifetime.

I remember being a new kid at school and a fellow fourth grader invited me to eat lunch with him. After we ate, we went to the playground and he introduced me to all of his friends. Although I don't remember that kid's name, he made me feel accepted and his act of kindness is something I have carried with me until this day.

God uses everyday people like him...and ordinary people just like you.

We have given power to a small group of people and we expect them to utilize our resources to initiate change. However this action creates a bottle neck and funds are often spent on providing programs for people who have heard the message a million times. The people that most need our message often feel offended by Christian culture because the financial investments show that we care more about our buildings and programs than we do about the harassed and helpless.

Servant leaders should be the catalyst for the faith; not the administrators of it. Jesus said:

My sheep listen to my voice; I know them,

and they follow me.

- John 10:27

This means that every follower of Jesus Christ is qualified to participate with him in the work of helping people reconcile in their intimate loving relationship with God. To learn more about how

CHRISTIANITY UNPLUGGED

you can live out your call to the ministry read of "Plan A - And there is no plan B" by Dwight Robertson.

Eric D. Canaday

- 4 -

A Revolution in Worship

You do not delight in sacrifice, or I would bring it; you do not take pleasure in burnt offerings. The sacrifices of God are a broken spirit; a broken and contrite heart, O God, you will not despise.

- Psalm 51:16-18

Eric D. Canaday

Christianity Unplugged

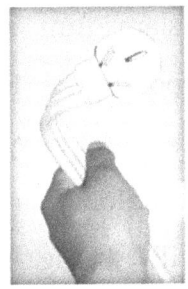

One night my son and I went to watch the Denver Nuggets play a basketball game at the Pepsi Center. I purchased our tickets, and spent an ungodly amount on concession food that was not all that great. Prior to the game, my wife bought my son a $60 nuggets Jersey so that he could be dressed like a member of the team. We went to our seats and within moments we were standing with our hands over our hearts listening to a beautiful rendition of the Star Spangled Banner. After the song was over we sat down comfortably in the seats ready to watch the spectacle.

We had a blast at the game. We cheered when Carmelo made a slam dunk and clapped when AI made a three point shot. But we never once considered that we might be able to sit courtside with the players, let alone play in the game. We were content with being spectators. Why? Because when they won, me and every other fan in that stadium felt like we won too. That feeling was worth the time and the dollars spent.

The same mentality is prevalent in today's worship services. The spectators are fans of Coach Jesus who enjoy sitting in the pews watching his small team of ordained clerics save souls from the pulpit. They have a Bible, a bumper sticker, and a Christian t-shirt. I used to be an active participant in these types of spectacles because I wanted:

- To hear and sing great music that was inspirational and culturally relevant.
- To listen to a "minister" who communicated the oracles of God with skill and passion
- To be able to give to a "ministry" where I

could see evidence that people are being saved (This was how I could measure my Return On Investment)
- To worship in a building that was comfortable, clean and pleasing to the eye.

Regarding this last point Rick Warren made the following comment in his article entitled "Six physical factors that affect your worship service"

Facilities and physical environment have a lot to do with what happens in a weekend worship service. The shape of your building will shape your service. Walk into some buildings and your mood will instantly brighten. Walk into other buildings and you'll feel depressed. The shape of a room can change a mood instantly; so can the temperature of room; so can the lighting in a room. Be aware of these factors and use them. Figure out what mood you want your service to project and then create it.

People go to parades, sporting events, arcades, concerts, movies, and worship services to enjoy the spectacle and to live their lives vicariously through the heroes who have committed to putting on the show. Today's church culture has made it acceptable to show up, sing a song, sit in the pew, put some money in the plate. This allows the attendees to sooth their conscience, and the money collected helps church leaders maintain their programs, facilities, and the theatrical experience that their members enjoy.

Without question Jesus performed spectacular miracles that drew large crowds. But he never utilized spectacles or singing as a vehicle for convincing people to passively watch the show that he and his team of ordained ministers performed each week. Jesus did not have a praise and worship team. He also made it clear that God does not require his children to gather in a centralized location each week for the purpose of worship. He explained this to a woman who was drawing water from a well. The woman said:

Christianity Unplugged

Sir...I can see that you are a prophet. Our fathers worshiped on this mountain, but you Jews claim that the place where we must worship is in Jerusalem." Jesus declared, "Believe me, woman, a time is coming when you will worship the Father neither on this mountain nor in Jerusalem. You Samaritans worship what you do not know; we worship what we do know, for salvation is from the Jews. Yet a time is coming and has now come when the true worshipers will worship the Father in spirit and truth, for they are the kind of worshipers the Father seeks. God is spirit, and his worshipers must worship in spirit and in truth - John 4:19-24

The temple in Jerusalem was constructed on Mount Moriah. This is significant because the first time the word worship was used in the bible was when God commanded Abraham to go to this location to offer a sacrifice. God manifested his presence in the Sanctuary of the temple and the priests would present sacrificial offerings to

God on the behalf of the people. Offerings were given to atone for the sins of the people. Tithes were given for the care of the temple, and the priest that served within it (see Numbers 18:21-28).

Jesus came to do away with the system of temple-based worship. Hebrews 9:24-28 explains how he did it:

> *For Christ did not enter a man-made sanctuary that was only a copy of the true one; he entered heaven itself, now to appear for us in God's presence. Nor did he enter heaven to offer himself again and again, the way the high priest enters the Most Holy Place every year with blood that is not his own. Then Christ would have had to suffer many times since the creation of the world. But now he has appeared once for all at the end of the ages to do away with sin by the sacrifice of himself. Just as man is destined to die once, and after that to face judgment, so Christ was sacrificed once to take away the sins of many people; and*

> *he will appear a second time, not to bear sin,*
> *but to bring salvation to those*
> *who are waiting for him.*

The truth is that Jesus died on the cross, and was buried. God raised him from the dead and he entered heaven itself and presented himself as the final sacrifice for sin. He now serves as our only High Priest and mediator before God. Because of this, we do not need a worship service, a temple, or an ordained minister to receive right standing with God. He sent the Spirit of God to dwell in the hearts of those who believe in him, which gives us the power to follow God's royal law of love.

God does not dwell in temples made with human hands! (see Acts 7:48-50). Anyone who knocks on your door and tells you that you have to go to a building or become a member of their group to be accepted by God is misled! Jesus taught us to worship in spirit and in truth...not in a sanctuary.

When I was a part of the system I always knew that the building was not the Church. I would always say that the Church was the people. But, I still believed that unaffiliated Christians were in spiritual danger because they did not participate in corporate worship and they did not have the protection that comes from being in "the house of God." This idea seemed spiritual. But it was not based in the truth.

Jesus has given God the ultimate sacrifice for sins on our behalf. God will not accept our time in the pews or our songs in the sanctuary as payment for our unloving behavior. He won't bless us on earth or reward us in heaven because of all of the souls that were saved through the ministries we finance. God wants us to follow his son by surrendering our lives in loving service to God and humanity.

There was a time when God required his people to worship him by presenting a sacrificial offering to a priest who served in "The House of God" (see Deuteronomy chapter 12). But Jesus came to do away with this system of worship. Romans 12:1 shows us how to worship God without a building or an ordained minister. It says:

> *Therefore, I urge you, brethren, in view of God's mercy, to offer your bodies as living sacrifices, holy and pleasing to God this is your spiritual act of worship.*

Ephesians 5:1-2 builds upon this:

> *Be imitators of God, therefore, as dearly loved children and live a life of love, just as Christ loved us and gave himself up for us as a fragrant offering and sacrifice to God.*

Jesus prioritized this revolutionary style of worship when he said:

> *As the Father has loved me, so have I loved you. Now remain in my love. If you obey my commands, you will remain in my love, just as I have obeyed my Father's commands and remain in his love. I have told you this so that my joy may be in you and that your joy may*

> *be complete. My command is this: Love each other as I have loved you. Greater love has no one than this, that he lay down his life for his friends. - John 15:9-13*

Praise and thanksgiving is an appropriate expression of our devotion to God. Even Jesus sang praises with his disciples (see Mathew 26:30). But singing, dancing, and lifting holy hands in a temple is not worship. Jesus modeled worship by laying down his life in loving service to humanity. He healed the sick, fed the poor, put his personal safety at risk by speaking the truth to power, and spent time with people who were suffering from emotional and spiritual oppression. If you are a follower of Jesus Christ he is leading you in worship by asking you to lay down your life in loving service to humanity through the work you do each day (The denominational/cultural divisions within the Church are proof positive that this kind of worship is imperative to the Church's role of being salt and light in the earth).

- 5 -

The Truth about Tithing

Each man should give what he has decided in his heart to give, not reluctantly or under compulsion, for God loves a cheerful giver.

- 2 Corinthians 9:7

Eric D. Canaday

CHRISTIANITY UNPLUGGED

Every Sunday thousands of preachers stand in front of their congregations and use Malachi 3:8-10 to scare their members into donating 10% of their income. It reads:

Will a man rob God? Yet you rob me. But you ask, 'How do we rob you?' In tithes and offerings. You are under a curse — the whole nation of you — because you are robbing me. Bring the whole tithe into the storehouse, that there may be food in my house. Test me in this," says the LORD Almighty, "and see if I will not throw open the floodgates of heaven and pour out so much blessing that you will not have room enough for it."

After the scripture is read someone will usually misapply it by stating that the local church is the storehouse and every member is obligated to comply with this legal requirement. Those who are faithful are told that God will open the windows of heaven and give them a financial blessing. Those who fail to tithe are given the impression that they are stealing from God and they will be punished with a financial curse. I have to say up front that I am not condemning the act of giving to worthy causes.

However, I am saying that teaching believers that they are obligated to tithe to the "local church" is both dishonest and misguided. Numbers 18:21-24 outlines the purpose of the tithe within the appropriate context. In it God says:

I give to the Levites all the tithes in Israel as their inheritance in return for the work they do while serving at the Tent of Meeting. From now on the Israelites must not go near the Tent of Meeting, or they will bear the consequences of their sin and will die. It is the Levites who are to do the work at the Tent of

> *Meeting and bear the responsibility for offenses against it. This is a lasting ordinance for the generations to come. They will receive no inheritance among the Israelites. Instead, I give to the Levites as their inheritance the tithes that the Israelites present as an offering to the LORD. That is why I said concerning them: 'They will have no inheritance among the Israelites.'*

The Levites were appointed by God to help the priests carry out their duties in the "House of God" (Numbers 18:1-7). The temple in Jerusalem was the storehouse that Malachi 3:8-10 refers to and it was the primary location where the nation's tithes could be presented (Deuteronomy 12:10-13). This temple was destroyed in 70 AD so there is not a storehouse where anyone has the authority to collect the tithe. Despite popular opinion, there is no biblical evidence that the local church building replaces the temple as the "House of God" (see 1 Chronicles 9:26-28, Acts 7:48-50, and Acts 17:24-25).

Further more, everyone who tithed in Israel was a landowner. In compliance with God's command, their tithe was a portion of the produce of the land that they owned (Deuteronomy 14:22). Most of the people who attend today's worship services are not landowners so they do not have any produce to give. The clerics demanding that tithes be paid do not work in the temple, and they are not descendents of Levi.

The Bible does encourage us to give generously and cheerfully (2 Corinthians 9:7). There is nothing wrong with collecting money in order to meet the needs of the people in your community. We all have the liberty to contribute any portion of our income wherever and to whomever we choose. But the truth is that believers have no spiritual obligation to tithe to the "local church".

If you have ever felt guilt, shame, or fear around the issue of tithing I want to tell you plainly that Jesus has paid every debt that you owe to God. If you are trying to give money as a way of receiving God's blessing, Jesus gave his life in vain. Galatians 3:10-14 settles the issue once and for all. It says:

> *All who rely on observing the law are under a curse, for it is written: 'Cursed is everyone who does not continue to do everything written in the Book of the Law.' Clearly no one is justified before God by the law, because, 'The righteous will live by faith.' The law is not based on faith; on the contrary, 'The man who does these things will live by them.' Christ redeemed us from the curse of the law by becoming a curse for us, for it is written: 'Cursed is everyone who is hung on a tree.' He redeemed us in order that the blessing given to Abraham might come to the Gentiles through Christ Jesus, so that by faith we might receive the promise of the Spirit.*

As a believer, the only spiritual debt that you have is to anyone is to love them (see Romans 13:8). Live free!

Eric D. Canaday

– 6 –

Getting Out of the Boat

For God has not given us a spirit of fear, but of power and of love and of a sound mind.

- 2 Timothy 1:7

Eric D. Canaday

CHRISTIANITY UNPLUGGED

Jesus had a cousin named John who was beheaded because he condemned the ruler of Galilee for marrying his brothers wife. When Jesus heard the news, he and the disciples decided to leave the towns where he had been preaching so that they could get a break from the crowds. They got into a boat and went to a solitary place. Unfortunately, the people found out about his plans and followed him by foot. When Jesus reached the lake shore there was a crowd of about 5,000 people waiting.

I am sure the disciples were disappointed because the primary reason that they left was so they could rest and reflect. But Jesus had compassion for the people. He knew that many of them were suffering in both body and spirit so he got out of the boat and healed the sick among them. Afterwards he fed them all and encouraged them to go back to the towns. As he was dispersing the crowd he made the disciples get back into the boat, telling them he would meet them on the other side the lake.

Jesus walked up the mountainside to pray for awhile. When he returned to the lake shore the disciples were a considerable distance away but they had not made it to the other side because the wind was against them. So he walked out on the water to meet them.

Matthew 14:26-31 says:

When the disciples saw him walking on the lake, they were terrified. "It's a ghost," they said, and cried out in fear. But Jesus immediately said to them:

"Take courage! It is I. Don't be afraid."

"Lord, if it's you," Peter replied,

"tell me to come to you on the water."

"Come," he said.

Then Peter got down out of the boat, walked on the water and came toward Jesus. But when he saw the wind, he was afraid and, beginning to sink, cried out, "Lord, save me!" Immediately Jesus reached out his hand and caught him. "You of little faith," he said, "why did you doubt?"

The boat was a safe place that was familiar to Peter. He was a fisherman by trade so he knew that as long as he was in the boat he would be secure. Christianity is much the same way. It provides safe places where we can participate in religious activities with very little risk or discomfort. But Jesus is inviting each of us to join him outside of the boat. He is calling every one of his followers to join him in the ministry of reconciliation.

Getting out of the boat does not necessarily mean that you need to abandon the community of believers that you are currently fellowshipping with.

But don't forget that there are people who pass by our worship facilities everyday uncertain if God really cares. They are aware of their shortcomings and they have heard about hell. They have considered going to a worship service, but have found more acceptance at the bar than from the Christians they know. These are the people the Jesus longs for.

Our practice of telling these people that they are going to burn forever hell if they don't accept Jesus or attend a worship service is like telling them you are going to hit them in the head with a baseball bat if they don't agree to come to your house for dinner. People are going through hell right now and they need to know that God wants to address the root cause of their suffering. Religion is not the answer. God's love working through your heart and hands is.

Fulfilling our mandate takes more than getting saved, going to a worship service, and putting money into an offering plate every week. It takes pastors and teachers who recognize that their job is to equip, not govern. It takes ordinary people who are not afraid to use their time, talent and treasure to address suffering and injustice in the world. It takes true believers who understand their obligation to love one another.

I understand that this is easier said than done because following Jesus takes courage, and many people choose religious activities because they are afraid or unwilling to do what he is asking. He called Peter out of the boat into troubled waters. He is also calling believers to step out of our religious constructs in order to follow him into the lives of people who may never come into our temples.

This is a daunting request in a narcissistic society where we are conditioned to pursue our own personal happiness. Still, in Matthew 10:37-39 Jesus said:

Anyone who loves his father or mother more than me is not worthy of me; anyone who loves his son or daughter more than me is not worthy of me; and anyone who does not take his cross and follow me is not worthy of me. Whoever finds his life will lose it, and whoever loses his life for my sake will find it.

What person living the American dream really has the time or the desire to pick up their cross and follow Jesus? And why should they when they can just pay the professionals to do it? Well the truth is that if we really want to follow Jesus the burden of being a minister of reconciliation who communicates the gospel and worships through loving self-sacrifice is ours to bear.

This process looks different for each of us so you may have to spend some time discovering how God wants you to follow Jesus in ways that are relevant to your talents, gifts, abilities, and life experiences. The impact that you make in the world is very closely tied to the work that you do each day. In light of that, here are a few books that may give you perspective as you step out the boat to follow Jesus into uncertain waters.

How to Find Your Mission in Life
by Richard N. Bolles

Christianity Unplugged

*Made to Count–Discovering
What toDo With Your Life*
by Bob Reccord & Randy Singer

*He Loves Me! Learning to Live
in the Father's Affection*
by Wayne Jacobsen

So You Don't Want to Go to Church Anymore
by Jake Colsen, Wayne Jacobsen,
and Dave Coleman

Eric D. Canaday

- 7 -

Life after Religion

It is for freedom that Christ has set us free. Stand firm, then, and do not let yourselves be burdened again by a yoke of slavery

- Galatians 5:1

Eric D. Canaday

CHRISTIANITY UNPLUGGED

When I lost my religion it was a struggle because it was extremely difficult for me to find other believers who were willing to have a dialogue about the challenges that we face in the Church. It seemed like every time I told my Christian friends that I was not a member of a local church, they immediately began trying to fix me. I explained my decision to one friend who responded by saying:

Eric that sounds like the spirit of offense. You must walk in forgiveness, overcome your hurt, and get back into the local church so that you can become the man of God that I know you are called to be.

Now, my friend hit the nail on the head when she said that I was offended, hurt, and struggling with forgiving the leaders within the system who were unwilling or unable to tell me the bare naked truth. I spent more than 25 years in Christianity believing that God would only love me if I served as a faithful cog in his religious machine. When I discovered this was not true, it took me another three years to overcome the disillusionment in a healthy way.

But, her reference to the "local church" alluded to the belief that every believer must remain in the arc of safety provided by the clerical authorities in order to be in right standing with God. This dynamic makes life outside of the boat difficult for those who are willing to challenge this notion. I wanted to maintain my relationships, but when I stepped away from the system, I had difficulty convincing many of my churchgoing friends to consider things from my point of view.

CHRISTIANITY UNPLUGGED

It took me some time to understand that it was not my job to convert them to my way of thinking. It is the Holy Spirit's job to convince people about the truth in God's word. My job is simply to share the truth in a loving way with those who are interested. If your journey is or will be similar to mine, here are a few steps that you can take to begin your life after religion.

FOLLOW JESUS

When I was a part of the system I was taught that the pastor of the local church was my "spiritual covering." What this means is that the pastor ruled over my spiritual life in Jesus' absence and I needed his permission to act as a representative of the church organization he governed. I am someone who wants "to be the change that I desire to see in the world," so my belief in being submitted to this type of authority created a lot of fear for me when I stepped out of the boat. I became free from this fear when I read 1 Timothy 2:5 which says:

There is one God and one mediator between God and humans, Jesus Christ.

What this means is that I do not have to go through a cleric or an organization to have a relationship with God or to be what He created me to be. Through Jesus I have direct access to God so there is no need for a middleman.

Again, mature believers are God's gift to the Church so learn from them. But you were not created to serve them. Their job is to serve you. Serve God, think for yourself, and follow Jesus into the lives of those he has created you to reach with his love.

Before I move on I have to pause and say there are some who will read this book that may think that Jesus Christ is insignificant or unnecessary. If you fall into that category, I want you to know that Jesus came to make the unknowable God *known* to mankind. There have been many teachers and prophets who have made claims about their spiritual knowledge but

Christianity Unplugged

Jesus made the bold claim of being the highest authority on everything pertaining to God. In Matthew 11:27-29 he said:

> *All things have been committed to me by my Father. No one knows the Son except the Father, and* **no one knows the Father except the Son and those to whom the Son chooses to reveal him.** *Come to me, all you who are weary and burdened, and I will give you rest. Take my yoke upon you and learn from me, for I am gentle and humble in heart, and you will find rest for your souls.*

Bottom line? If you are really serious about knowing God and developing an intimate loving relationship with Him, Jesus Christ can show you how. *He is the true way to enlightenment* (see John 14:6-7). Follow him and his teachings revealed in the Bible.

LIVE A LIFE OF LOVE

For me, Christianity was nothing more than a bunch of rules that I had to keep in order to avoid God's wrath. I have learned that God loves me more than I will ever love my own children. I don't have to live in fear of Him if I walk in his grace and live in his love. 1 John 4:16 states that "God is love." However, the word love has been so misused that I think it is important to provide a clear definition. 1 Corinthians 13 lets us know that...

> *Love is patient and kind. It does not envy and it is not boastful or proud. It is not rude or selfish. It is not easily angered and it forgives when wronged. Love does not delight in the harm of others but rejoices with the truth. It always protects, always trusts, always hopes, and always perseveres. Love never fails...And now these three remain: faith, hope and love. But the greatest of these is love.*

Please do not treat this definition as a list of rules to be followed! Once we place our faith in Jesus

Christianity Unplugged

Christ God pours his love into our heart through His Spirit to empower us with the ability to live out this lofty ideal. Our job is to allow him to transform our hearts as we make a conscious decision to make love our highest ambition. Galatians 5:16-23 shows us what this looks like. It says:

...live by the Spirit, and you will not gratify the desires of the unloving nature. For the unloving nature desires what is contrary to the Spirit, and the Spirit what is contrary to the unloving nature. They are in conflict with each other, so that you do not do what you want.

But if you are led by the Spirit, you are not under law.

The acts of the unloving nature are obvious: sexual immorality, impurity and debauchery; idol worship and witchcraft; hatred, discord, jealousy, fits of rage, selfish ambition, dissensions, factions and envy; drunkenness, orgies, and the like. I warn you, as I did before,

> *that those who live like this will not inherit the kingdom of God.*
>
> *But the fruit of the Spirit is love, joy, peace, patience, kindness, goodness, faithfulness, gentleness and self-control. Against such things there is no law.*

Again following Jesus is not about following rules. It is all about being transformed from the inside out by his love, and then sharing that transformation with the world.

Study the Scriptures

Life is hectic and it is difficult to set aside time to study the scriptures. When I was attending worship services I knew that I could skip my personal bible study because I could rely on the preacher to give me the Cliff Notes of his weekly studies on Sunday morning.

The problem with this approach to the Bible is that it trains us to allow others to think for us. I was ticked off when I discovered the truth about God. But I got over my anger when I accepted the fact that I had a Bible that I was not reading. My ignorance was my fault and it was unreasonable for me to place the blame on clerics who may not have known the truth themselves.

So that you know, the Bible is not a manual or a rulebook. There are laws in the bible, but they were given to govern people who were unwilling or unable to love each other from the heart. What we call the "Old Testament" provides a history of one nation's struggle with following the way of God. What we call the "New Testament" reveals God's plan to redeem that nation and the world by providing justice and grace through his son Jesus the Messiah. But don't take my word for it...read it for yourself. If reading is not your thing then buy the CD or MP3 version and listen to it.

GET DIRECTION THROUGH PRAYER

Prayer used to be a chore because I could never really figure out why God would want to hear anything I had to say. I also believed that the preacher was the oracle that God spoke through, so I had little expectation that I could hear from God unless it came from the pulpit. I know that might sound ridiculous to you, but this kind of thinking is what defined my prayer life.

Now I know that God loves me and he has a plan for my life that doesn't have anything to do with someone else's vision or mission statement. Ephesians 2:10 says that

> *We are God's workmanship, created in Christ Jesus to do good works, which God prepared in advance for us to do.*

From the pulpit you can learn about the good works that the preacher has prepared for you. From the Bible you can see how God was at work in the lives of others. Through prayer you can discover how to become everything that God created you to be.

Prayer is an act of humility that acknowledges that we don't have all of the answers. It is a time where we can ask God how we can use our talents gifts and abilities to share his love with others in a relevant way. During prayer we can tell God about all of our cares and concerns like a child sitting in the arms of a loving father. There is no prescribed formula for prayer so you can communicate with God through the words of your mouth or through the meditations of your heart. A prayer can be a heartfelt thank you or a song of thanksgiving that you put to music and share with the world!

When God responds to your prayers it will likely come to you as an intuitive insight or a burst of knowledge that I call an "ah-ha" moment. God frequently speaks to me in this way and as you develop the habit of praying and meditating on his word revealed in the bible, I believe that you will be lead by the Spirit of God in similar ways.

God is our father. He is not a magical genie that answers at our beck and call. There will be times when it seems that God is silent. Don't freak out and assume that God has abandoned you because we have a promise that he will never leave us or forsake us (see Hebrews 13:5 and Romans 8:28-39). Like our earthly parents and mentors, sometimes God wants for us to apply the lessons that he has already taught us. It may help you to keep a journal were you can document and revisit the things that you are learning during your times with God.

If you have never really prayed before, there is a prayer that Jesus taught to his disciples in Matthew 6:9-13 that may help. I highly encourage you to read the text for yourself, but I have provided a modified version of the prayer below to give you an example of how you can make it personal.

Hey Dad, I acknowledge you as the creator of the universe and there is no one I can compare to you. Things are a little crazy in our world, so I ask you to send your Son back soon to establish your love in our hearts and bring peace to every nation on the earth. There are so many things that I want, but today I ask you to give me what I need. There are people who have done me wrong but forgive me the same way that I forgive them. It's possible that I may be tempted to do things that I know are not a part of your plan for me. So please help me steer clear of anything that would cause harm to me or someone else. Love ya' Dad...thanks for everything!

Prayer and meditation give us direct access to God. However, there are many unhealthy sources of spiritual knowledge out there. Be sure to use reason, common sense, and the pattern of God's character revealed in the scripture as you learn to hear and respond to God's leading.

Connect to Community

A temple is a place where you bring an offering to a priest so that God will forgive you for the wrongs you have done. Jesus did away with this system by offering his life on the altar of the cross (for insight on this read the entire book of Hebrews). Because of this we are under no obligation to attend a weekly "worship service."

Still, God has created us for community. Better stated, when we accepted Jesus as the commander and chief of our life we not only became members of his kingdom, we also became members of his family. In the scriptures this family is called the Church. The word Church is the English translation of the Greek word ekklesia, which literally means "assembly." 1 Peter 2:9-10 gives a description of this assembly:

But you are a chosen people, a royal priesthood, a holy nation, a people belonging to God, that you may declare the praises of him who called you out of darkness into his wonderful light. Once you were not a people, but now you are the people of God; once you had not received mercy, but now you have received mercy.

The Church is not a building that you can go to or an event you can attend. It is a worldwide family that we become a part of when we devote or loyalty to Jesus Christ. He is the head of this family and he governs it through the Spirit of God in our hearts. Faith in God's son Jesus Christ and authentic love is the glue that binds this family together.

This concept of Church was foreign to me. I grew up in a single parent home with very few ties to an extended family. My connections to religious communities were based upon obligation and I have had very few people in my life that I felt like I could really trust. After I walked away from institutional Christianity I did not want to participate in anything that reminded me of my experiences there. However, Hebrews 10:23-32 says:

> *Let us hold unswervingly to the hope we profess, for he who promised is faithful. And let us consider how we may spur one another on toward love and good deeds. Let us not give up meeting together, as some are in the habit of doing, but let us encourage one another –*

and all the more as you see the Day approaching.

Jesus came not only to connect us in relationship to the Father. He also came to connect us in loving relationships with one another. He was so serious about this that he said that the way that his followers could be recognized is by their love for one another (see John 13:34-35, Rom. 12:10 & 13:8). Hebrews admonishes us to assemble together for the purposes of "encouragement" and to "spur one another on towards love and good deeds".

Acts 2:42 lets us know that when the first members of the Church gathered, they devoted themselves to:

- the apostles' teaching (reading and discussing the Bible)
- the fellowship (hanging out with the family),
- the breaking of bread (sharing meals/Lord's Supper together)
- and to prayer.

Talking, hanging out, eating, and praying is not something that is difficult to do. It can happen at a coffee shop with one or two others, or it can happen within the context of a barbeque that someone holds in their home. The goal is growing in God's love and being mutually encouraged to be what he has created us to be.

I have found that connecting to community can be a slow process because many believers only understand Church within the context of a temple-based worship service led by an ordained minister. At minimum, I suggest that you begin meeting with no less than two other believers as frequently as you feel led, who will uplift you in your daily walk with God. As you open yourself up to being an active part of the family, God will begin networking you into deeper connections within the body.

Beware of the religious desire to start a gathering and then create a bunch of rules to force people to participate. Jesus is perfectly capable of knitting the family together how he sees fit. So find ways to get connected where ever and to whomever he leads you to. The key is personal accountability through a few close relationships where you have open discussions about life, love, work, and faith in action.

Let go of
Bitterness and Resentment

There are quite a few well-meaning church folks who have hurt people thinking they were doing God's work. I have seen people shunned for wearing the "wrong" clothes, or ridiculed for doing something as simple as chewing gum in "the sanctuary."

If you have ever been hurt by Christians I am sure your feelings are probably legitimate. However, you cannot be a victor and victim at the same time. Scripture encourages us to forgive others the way that we want to be forgiven (see Matthew 6:12)

Forgiving the people that have disappointed you does not mean that they get off scott-free. It also does not mean that you must continue to let people take advantage of you. However, when you forgive those who have hurt you, what you are doing is transferring the responsibility of judgment to God. Romans 12:17-19,21 says:

> *Do not repay anyone evil for evil. Be careful to do what is right in the eyes of everybody. If it is possible, as far as it depends on you, live at peace with everyone. Do not take revenge, my friends, but leave room for God's wrath, for it is written: "It is mine to avenge; I will repay," says the Lord...Do not be overcome by evil, but overcome evil with good.*

I held on to bitterness and resentment because it was my way of punishing those who had hurt me. But Job 36:13 says "The godless in heart harbor resentment." What this meant for me is that I could not mature God's love while I was justifying the hatred in my heart (see 1 John 4:19-21). I wanted to live free in God's love so I forgave those who had hurt me and moved on.

If you are holding on to bitterness and resentment I highly encourage you to let it go.

Even though there are significant problems with Christianity, God does not expect us to live out our faith as lone rangers. It is vitally important that we maintain a close relationship with Him and other believers as we follow His Son beyond the construct of religion.

I wrote this book in hopes of helping believers overcome the barriers that stand in the way of following Jesus. My hope is that the Church will move beyond human-based denominational ministry into the relational ministry of reconciliation lead by Jesus Christ, the Son of God.

If you are pastor reading this book, I pray that you will devote your life to equipping every believer for the ministry even if it means that you must give up personal prestige or clerical power. To everyone reading this book my prayer is that you will overcome fear, step out of the boat and

Christianity Unplugged

follow Jesus into places where only God's power can keep you afloat. If you need encouragement, support, or you want to share all that God is doing in your life please join the conversation we are having at www.christianityunplugged.net .

Eric D. Canaday

– Epilogue –

You don't have to be perfect

... "My grace is sufficient for you, for my power is made perfect in weakness." Therefore I will boast all the more gladly about my weaknesses, so that Christ's power may rest on me.

2 Corinthians 12:9

Eric D. Canaday

Christianity Unplugged

In November of 2006 my father was diagnosed with terminal liver cancer. When the doctor gave us the news I was stunned, but I can't say that I was surprised. You see, for as long as I can remember, my father used alcohol as a way of coping with the demons of his past. For this reason (and others), we were never really that close. Still, I always loved him and I didn't want him to be alone during his final days on the earth.

After discussing the situation, my wife and I made the decision to provide hospice care for him in our home. He died on Thanksgiving Day, about two weeks after he was diagnosed. It was one of the most trying experiences of my life, but

I was grateful that he was able to transition peacefully amongst family and friends.

My father developed a strong faith in Jesus Christ during his latter years so I am certain that things are better for him now. But sadly, he lived most of his earthly life in turmoil because he never realized just how much his life really mattered.

From what I have seen and heard, his mother was a lot like the foster mother depicted in the movie Antwone Fisher. His father was never an active part of his life, and he was consistently forced into the role of being the caregiver for his younger siblings. His daughter distrusted him almost until the time that he passed away. My mother divorced him because of infidelity and his second wife left him because of his drinking problem. He died with $45 dollars in his bank account, minimal assets, and no insurance policy. By all worldly accounts he was a failure.

However, at his wake I met people from his past and present who were profoundly impacted by the love he shared with them during everyday encounters. At his funeral, people spoke of him as if he had been a Nobel Peace Prize winner.

I never really thought much of him when he was alive. I think he had trouble thinking very highly of himself. But as I listened to the remarks being given about my dad I learned a valuable lesson:

God uses imperfect people because there aren't any perfect people around. 1 Corinthians 1:25-27 says:

> *For the foolishness of God is wiser than man's wisdom, and the weakness of God is stronger than man's strength. Brothers, think of what you were when you were called. Not many of you were wise by human standards; not many were influential; not many were of noble birth. But God chose the foolish things of the world to shame the wise; God chose the weak things of the world to shame the strong."*

Eric D. Canaday

In arrogance, I thought of myself as better than my dad. In his dying, I was brought to my knees by the realization that he was someone to be respected and admired. He was not perfect…but he made a mark on this world that I believe will be recorded in the annals of eternity.

I received the following letter in the mail after my father's funeral. It is a testament to his legacy and I pray that it will inspire you to transform the world in ways that look like you.

Dear Eric,

Your father was a cherished friend. We met over two years ago when I approached him about providing care for the old mansion and grounds at the rape crisis center I manage. Two years is merely a blink in a lifetime, yet knowing your father changed my life in ways difficult to explain.

At his service today, I was grinning when you and Mr. Stovall noted his early morning

Christianity Unplugged

"connections." I, too, am a very early morning person, arriving at the office around 6:00-6:30 each morning. Don knew the coffee would be on and he'd often pop in to fill his mug, or sit and chat for a bit before he tackled his day's agenda.

Those conversations are precious to me. Your father was a great educator. I refer to him as a political scientist and historian. We talked history (rather he did, while I learned), politics, race relations, sports, music, spirituality, and even addictive illness.

I mention that because your father was a great humanitarian. I never, ever, heard him say an unkind thing about anyone. He spoke so fondly of you and Simone, his grandchildren, and his church community. And he always went the extra mile in his work, without expectation of notice or reward.

In an office of 20+ women, Don was like an anchor for us; a man we trusted, admired, enjoyed immensely, and depended upon. He was the epitome of respect and goodwill. His passing rocked our agency. I still look for his white van each morning.

Eric, I know your father had demons he fought probably most of his life. That could not have been easy for you and your sister...family dynamics are so complicated. But what touched me deeply was your father's determination to keep trying to do what was right. That was inspiring. He lived fully, yet humbly.

I want to add one more thing. In the courtyard of our office building was a pathetic hibiscus plant no one took the time to care for -- until your father entered out lives. He nurtured that plant for two years to produce magnificent, stunning, enormous blooms! What a lovely legacy he has left for our clients who come for trauma recovery and for those of us who need frequent reminders of the beauty in life. Each spring and summer as those blossoms unfold, I will feel your father's presence and celebrate the richness of his extraordinary spirit...

www.ingramcontent.com/pod-product-compliance
Lightning Source LLC
Chambersburg PA
CBHW071300040426
42444CB00009B/1796